BELIEVE IN YOURSELF YOU ARE

Amazing

summersdale

BELIEVE IN YOURSELF, YOU ARE AMAZING

Summersdale Publishers Ltd
46 West Street
Chichester
West Sussex
PO19 1RP
UK

www.summersdale.com

Printed and bound in the Czech Republic

ISBN: 978-1-84953-717-9

Substantial discounts on bulk quantities of Summersdale books are available to corporations, professional associations and other organisations. For details contact general enquiries: telephone: +44 (0) 1243 771107, fax: +44 (0) 1243 786300 or email: enquiries@summersdale.com.

TO......................................

FROM.................................

THE SECRET OF GETTING AHEAD IS GETTING STARTED.

Mark Twain

You can change the world

START WHERE YOU ARE.
USE WHAT YOU HAVE.
DO WHAT YOU CAN.

Arthur Ashe

DON'T WATCH THE CLOCK; DO WHAT IT DOES. KEEP GOING.

Sam Levenson

IT IS OUR CHOICES...
THAT SHOW WHAT WE
TRULY ARE, FAR MORE
THAN OUR ABILITIES.

J. K. Rowling

Nothing is impossible

EVEN IF YOU FALL ON YOUR FACE, YOU'RE STILL MOVING FORWARD.

Victor Kiam

EXPECT PROBLEMS
AND EAT THEM
FOR BREAKFAST.

Alfred A. Montapert

If you can't do it, no one can

PROBLEMS ARE NOT STOP SIGNS. THEY ARE GUIDELINES.

Robert H. Schuller

WHAT YOU PLANT NOW, YOU WILL HARVEST LATER.

Og Mandino

YOU ARE NEVER TOO OLD TO SET ANOTHER GOAL OR TO DREAM A NEW DREAM.

C. S. Lewis

Go for it

ORDINARY ME CAN ACHIEVE SOMETHING EXTRAORDINARY BY GIVING THAT LITTLE BIT EXTRA.

Bear Grylls

WITH THE NEW DAY COMES NEW STRENGTH AND NEW THOUGHTS.

Eleanor Roosevelt

Positivity is
contagious

CREATE THE KIND OF SELF THAT YOU WILL BE HAPPY TO LIVE WITH ALL YOUR LIFE.

Golda Meir

STEP BY STEP
AND THE THING
IS DONE.

Charles Atlas

DON'T GIVE UP.
DON'T LOSE HOPE.
DON'T SELL OUT.

Christopher Reeve

Mountains
are there to be
climbed

FAITH IS TAKING THE FIRST STEP EVEN WHEN YOU DON'T SEE THE WHOLE STAIRCASE.

Martin Luther King Jr

DO NOT WAIT TO STRIKE TILL THE IRON IS HOT; BUT MAKE IT HOT BY STRIKING.

William Butler Yeats

Don't let other
people live
your life

EVERYONE'S DREAM CAN COME TRUE IF YOU JUST STICK TO IT AND WORK HARD.

Serena Williams

NEVER GIVE IN — NEVER, NEVER, NEVER, NEVER.

Winston Churchill

ONLY THOSE WHO NEVER STEP, NEVER STUMBLE.

Richard Paul Evans

Be your own
cheerleader

DON'T THINK LIMITS.

Usain Bolt

WHAT YOU DO TODAY CAN IMPROVE ALL YOUR TOMORROWS.

Ralph Marston

If you're
too short to
reach... jump
a little higher

IT IS ONLY BY BEING BOLD THAT YOU GET ANYWHERE.

Richard Branson

PERSEVERANCE IS NOT
A LONG RACE; IT IS
MANY SHORT RACES ONE
AFTER THE OTHER.

Walter Elliot

BIG SHOTS ARE ONLY LITTLE SHOTS WHO KEEP SHOOTING.

Christopher Morley

It's only a
problem if you
make it one

MAN'S CREATIVE STRUGGLE, HIS SEARCH FOR WISDOM AND TRUTH, IS A LOVE STORY.

Iris Murdoch

WE LEARN FROM FAILURE, NOT FROM SUCCESS!

Bram Stoker

Be the master
of your destiny

THERE IS ALWAYS
ROOM AT THE TOP.

Daniel Webster

ONE FINDS LIMITS BY PUSHING THEM.

Herbert Simon

THE PAST CANNOT BE CHANGED. THE FUTURE IS YET IN YOUR POWER.

Hugh White

Winding paths
lead to the most
interesting
places

WHEN YOU COME TO A ROAD BLOCK, TAKE A DETOUR.

Mary Kay Ash

MARCH ON, AND FEAR NOT THE THORNS, OR THE SHARP STONES ON LIFE'S PATH.

Kahlil Gibran

If your dreams
run, chase them

OPPORTUNITY DOES NOT KNOCK. IT PRESENTS ITSELF WHEN YOU BEAT DOWN THE DOOR.

Kyle Chandler

I CAN, THEREFORE I AM.

Simone Weil

NOTHING IS IMPOSSIBLE.
THE WORD ITSELF SAYS
'I'M POSSIBLE'!

Audrey Hepburn

Your life is a book. Make every chapter count

BELIEVE YOU CAN AND YOU'RE HALFWAY THERE.

Theodore Roosevelt

IT IS NOT THE MOUNTAIN WE CONQUER, BUT OURSELVES.

Edmund Hillary

*Sometimes
you have to
jump hurdles
to win a race*

WE MUST HAVE PERSEVERANCE AND ABOVE ALL CONFIDENCE IN OURSELVES.

Marie Curie

WHEN YOU HAVE CONFIDENCE, YOU CAN HAVE A LOT OF FUN.

Joe Namath

WHETHER YOU COME FROM A COUNCIL ESTATE OR A COUNTRY ESTATE, YOUR SUCCESS WILL BE DETERMINED BY YOUR OWN CONFIDENCE.

Michelle Obama

You are a hero

IF YOU'RE PRESENTING YOURSELF WITH CONFIDENCE, YOU CAN PULL OFF PRETTY MUCH ANYTHING.

Katy Perry

TO LOVE ONESELF IS THE BEGINNING OF A LIFE-LONG ROMANCE.

Oscar Wilde

Go you!

I'VE FINALLY STOPPED RUNNING AWAY FROM MYSELF. WHO ELSE IS THERE BETTER TO BE?

Goldie Hawn

TO BE YOURSELF IN A WORLD THAT IS CONSTANTLY TRYING TO MAKE YOU SOMETHING ELSE IS THE GREATEST ACCOMPLISHMENT.

Ralph Waldo Emerson

AS SOON AS YOU TRUST YOURSELF, YOU WILL KNOW HOW TO LIVE.

Johann Wolfgang von Goethe

Take time
to be silly

YOU ARE BRAVER THAN YOU
BELIEVE, STRONGER THAN
YOU SEEM, AND SMARTER
THAN YOU THINK.

A. A. Milne

IT'S ALWAYS TOO EARLY TO QUIT.

Norman Vincent Peale

There's nothing
you can't handle

YOUR CHANCES OF SUCCESS IN ANY UNDERTAKING CAN ALWAYS BE MEASURED BY YOUR BELIEF IN YOURSELF.

Robert Collier

OPTIMISM IS THE FAITH THAT LEADS TO ACHIEVEMENT.

Helen Keller

IF YOU'RE GOING THROUGH HELL, KEEP GOING.

Winston Churchill

Be bold enough
to cross the line.

LISTEN TO YOUR HEART
ABOVE ALL OTHER VOICES.

Marta Kagan

ALWAYS BE A FIRST-RATE
VERSION OF YOURSELF,
INSTEAD OF A SECOND-RATE
VERSION OF SOMEBODY ELSE.

Judy Garland

Reach for
the sky

SELF-TRUST IS THE FIRST SECRET OF SUCCESS.

Ralph Waldo Emerson

ALL GREAT ACHIEVEMENTS
REQUIRE TIME.

Maya Angelou

KEEP YOUR EYES ON THE STARS, AND YOUR FEET ON THE GROUND.

Theodore Roosevelt

It's yours for
the taking

I WAS ALWAYS LOOKING
OUTSIDE MYSELF FOR
STRENGTH AND CONFIDENCE
BUT IT COMES FROM WITHIN.

Anna Freud

IT'S WHERE WE GO, AND
WHAT WE DO WHEN WE
GET THERE, THAT TELLS
US WHO WE ARE.

Joyce Carol Oates

*Show the world
what you're
made of*

CONFIDENCE COMES NOT FROM ALWAYS BEING RIGHT, BUT FROM NOT FEARING TO BE WRONG.

Peter McIntyre

NOTHING SPLENDID HAS EVER BEEN ACHIEVED EXCEPT BY THOSE WHO DARED BELIEVE... SOMETHING INSIDE OF THEM WAS SUPERIOR TO CIRCUMSTANCE.

Bruce Fairchild Barton

THE BEST WAY TO GAIN SELF-CONFIDENCE IS TO DO WHAT YOU ARE AFRAID TO DO.

Anonymous

Conquer
your
doubt

LIFE IS A GREAT BIG CANVAS, AND YOU SHOULD THROW ALL THE PAINT ON IT YOU CAN.

Danny Kaye

OPPORTUNITIES DON'T OFTEN COME ALONG. SO, WHEN THEY DO, YOU HAVE TO GRAB THEM.

Audrey Hepburn

If an opportunity arises, don't hesitate

LOVE IS THE GREAT MIRACLE-CURE. LOVING OURSELVES WORKS MIRACLES IN OUR LIVES.

Louise Hay

HE HAS ACHIEVED SUCCESS WHO HAS LIVED WELL, LAUGHED OFTEN AND LOVED MUCH.

Bessie Anderson Stanley

NEVER BEND YOUR HEAD. ALWAYS HOLD IT HIGH. LOOK THE WORLD STRAIGHT IN THE EYE.

Helen Keller

Make your
dreams a reality

HAPPINESS IS THE SECRET TO ALL BEAUTY; THERE IS NO BEAUTY THAT IS ATTRACTIVE WITHOUT HAPPINESS.

Christian Dior

DON'T BE AFRAID TO GO OUT ON A LIMB. THAT'S WHERE THE FRUIT IS.

E. C. McKenzie

You're the boss

PLUNGE BOLDLY INTO THE
THICK OF LIFE, AND SEIZE
IT WHERE YOU WILL, IT IS
ALWAYS INTERESTING.

Johann Wolfgang von Goethe

DARE TO LOVE YOURSELF AS IF YOU WERE A RAINBOW WITH GOLD AT BOTH ENDS.

Aberjhani

THE TIDE TURNS AT LOW WATER AS WELL AS AT HIGH.

Havelock Ellis

The show
must go on

EVERY DAY BRINGS A
CHANCE FOR YOU TO DRAW
IN A BREATH, KICK OFF YOUR
SHOES... AND DANCE.

Oprah Winfrey

BE YOURSELF; EVERYONE ELSE IS ALREADY TAKEN.

Oscar Wilde

Follow your dreams

COURAGE IS NOT THE
ABSENCE OF FEAR, BUT
RATHER THE JUDGEMENT
THAT SOMETHING ELSE
IS MORE IMPORTANT
THAN FEAR.

Meg Cabot

THE EASIEST COURAGE IS THE
SORT THAT YOU WANT WHEN
YOU HAVEN'T GOT THINGS.

Hugh Walpole

IF MY MIND CAN CONCEIVE IT, AND MY HEART CAN BELIEVE IT, I KNOW I CAN ACHIEVE IT.

Jesse Jackson

Never give up

A GREAT LEADER'S COURAGE TO FULFIL HIS VISION COMES FROM PASSION, NOT POSITION.

John Maxwell

A SHIP IS SAFE IN HARBOUR, BUT THAT'S NOT WHAT SHIPS ARE FOR.

William Greenough Thayer Shedd

The higher you jump, the closer you get

YOUR WILLINGNESS TO WRESTLE WITH YOUR DEMONS WILL CAUSE YOUR ANGELS TO SING.

August Wilson

SOMETIMES COURAGE IS THE
QUIET VOICE AT THE END OF
THE DAY SAYING 'I WILL TRY
AGAIN TOMORROW.'

Mary Anne Radmacher

TOUGHNESS IS IN THE SOUL AND SPIRIT, NOT IN MUSCLES.

Alex Karras

Trust in
yourself

COURAGE IS RESISTANCE TO FEAR, MASTERY OF FEAR — NOT ABSENCE OF FEAR.

Mark Twain

COURAGE IS WHAT IT
TAKES TO STAND UP AND
SPEAK; COURAGE IS ALSO
WHAT IT TAKES TO SIT
DOWN AND LISTEN.

· Winston Churchill

There's always
a way

BE BRAVE. TAKE RISKS.
NOTHING CAN SUBSTITUTE
EXPERIENCE.

Paulo Coelho

HE WHO MOVES
NOT FORWARD,
GOES BACKWARD.

Johann Wolfgang von Goethe

COURAGE IS THE ART OF BEING THE ONLY ONE WHO KNOWS YOU'RE SCARED TO DEATH.

Earl Wilson

Rise to the
challenge

YOU WILL NEVER DO
ANYTHING IN THIS WORLD
WITHOUT COURAGE. IT IS THE
GREATEST QUALITY OF THE
MIND NEXT TO HONOUR.

Aristotle

START BY DOING WHAT'S NECESSARY; THEN DO WHAT'S POSSIBLE; AND SUDDENLY YOU ARE DOING THE IMPOSSIBLE.

Francis of Assisi

Be the
superhero in
your story

IT'S THE JOB THAT'S NEVER STARTED AS TAKES LONGEST TO FINISH.

J. R. R. Tolkien

HAPPINESS IS A MATTER
OF ONE'S MOST ORDINARY
AND EVERYDAY MODE
OF CONSCIOUSNESS
BEING... LIVELY AND
UNCONCERNED WITH SELF.

Iris Murdoch

ANYTHING'S POSSIBLE IF YOU'VE GOT ENOUGH NERVE.

J. K. Rowling

Goals are only
achievable if
you set them in
the first place

PERSEVERANCE IS FAILING NINETEEN TIMES AND SUCCEEDING THE TWENTIETH.

Julie Andrews

ALWAYS BEAR IN MIND THAT
YOUR OWN RESOLUTION
TO SUCCEED IS MORE
IMPORTANT THAN ANY
OTHER ONE THING.

Abraham Lincoln

*Show doubt
what you're
made of*

NEVER GIVE UP! FAILURE AND REJECTION ARE ONLY THE FIRST STEP TO SUCCEEDING.

Jim Valvano

MY ATTITUDE IS THAT IF YOU PUSH ME TOWARDS... A WEAKNESS... I WILL TURN THAT PERCEIVED WEAKNESS INTO A STRENGTH.

Michael Jordan

DEFEAT IS NOT THE WORST OF FAILURES. NOT TO HAVE TRIED IS THE TRUE FAILURE.

George Edward Woodberry

*You're
unstoppable*

EVERY MORNING STARTS A NEW PAGE IN YOUR STORY. MAKE IT A GREAT ONE TODAY.

Doe Zantamata

SUCCESS SEEMS TO BE
LARGELY A MATTER OF
HANGING ON AFTER
OTHERS HAVE LET GO.

William Feather

You have the power

WE HAVE A HOPE OF SUCCEEDING IF WE LEARN FROM OUR PAST MISTAKES.

Carl Levin

SUCCESS IS NOT FINAL,
FAILURE IS NOT FATAL:
IT IS THE COURAGE TO
CONTINUE THAT COUNTS.

Winston Churchill

NEVER GIVE UP ON WHAT YOU REALLY WANT TO DO.

Albert Einstein

Give it your all

BE SO GOOD THEY CAN'T IGNORE YOU.

Steve Martin

CHAMPIONS KEEP PLAYING UNTIL THEY GET IT RIGHT.

Billie Jean King

Be the best

AIM FOR THE MOON. IF YOU MISS, YOU MAY HIT A STAR.

W. Clement Stone

DON'T COMPARE YOURSELF
WITH ANYONE IN THIS
WORLD... IF YOU DO SO, YOU
ARE INSULTING YOURSELF.

Bill Gates

THERE IS NO GREATER THING YOU CAN DO WITH YOUR LIFE AND YOUR WORK THAN FOLLOW YOUR PASSIONS.

Richard Branson

Chase your
dreams

MAKE THE MOST OF
YOURSELF BY FANNING THE
TINY, INNER SPARKS OF
POSSIBILITY INTO FLAMES
OF ACHIEVEMENT.

Golda Meir

IF YOU RISK NOTHING, YOU GAIN NOTHING.

Bear Grylls

You can do it!

IF YOU CAN FIND A
PATH WITH NO OBSTACLES,
IT PROBABLY DOESN'T
LEAD ANYWHERE.

Frank A. Clark

WE NEED TO BE CONFIDENT. WE NEED NOT TO BLINK.

Sebastian Coe

WE NEED TO LEARN TO LOVE OURSELVES FIRST, IN ALL OUR GLORY AND OUR IMPERFECTIONS.

John Lennon

Spending a minute with you makes my day

BEWARE; FOR I AM FEARLESS, AND THEREFORE POWERFUL.

Mary Shelley

IF YOU FELL DOWN YESTERDAY, STAND UP TODAY.

H. G. Wells

ONLY IN THE DARKNESS CAN YOU SEE THE STARS.

Martin Luther King Jr

José is a fun-loving, free-wheeling owl who
believes in seizing the day and the power of
self-belief! He travels the world, spreading cheer
and positivity through his uplifting books.

For more information about our books,
find us on Facebook at **Summersdale Publishers**
and follow us on Twitter at **@Summersdale.**

www.summersdale.com